POEMS FROM GOD

By

Paul R. Cantrell

xulon PRESS

To
Virginia
May the peace of God follow
you all through your life
Bless You

Paul Cantrell

7-1-07

I dedicate this book to the memory of my mother Opal Cantrell, who lived Christ before me. Also to my daughter Tamara, may it reveal to her the fact that Christ Jesus is Lord.
I want to thank Cheryl who first put it in book form as a Christmas present, and Tati for all her hours of hard work to bring it all together as the work you hold in your hands.

TESTIMONIAL

I am a firm believer that one cannot give away what one does not posses, or at least one should not. One of the greatest encouragements to me concerning Paul's book is that it is written on his heart. Paul possesses the understanding of the character of God that is depicted in the pages of his writings. Many of the poems/proverbs in this collection span many years and much of the journey the Lord Jesus has had Paul on. Yet, almost without warning, you can speak to him on a subject which he as pinned, and he will immediately recall what he describes as "what the Lord gave me." He can also tell you when and where he most likely was, both geographically and in his life's journey, when the Lord gave it to him.

The scriptures tell us that we overcome by the Blood of the Lamb and by the Word of our testimony. I have always held that the Blood of the Lamb is God's part more believable at times. In the sense that it carries us from the abstractly possible to the "it's probable even for me." In this sense if He did it "here", a specific time and place we can point too, and in that if He did the same for someone else, then reality is placed within our hope that He can do it for me.

As you read Paul's book I know that you will gain strength and encouragement for your journey. You will know that because God pulled Paul through the tough times, led him along the smooth and rocky paths, that you can trust him to do the same for you.

Pastor Timothy T. Corder

TABLE OF CONTENTS

The Pen

Father, You are the poet,
I am the pen.
I know that they're Your words,
From the beginning to the end.

I'm humbled that You have chosen
To use me in this way.
That thru my pen, you'll let the world
Know what you have to say.

Help me be faithful to listen to You.
And write it down with ink and pen,
And through Your words that I've written down,
May the world want to seek you again.

The Cornerstone

The Lord is the cornerstone
On which to build your life upon,
For once you have the foundation laid
The life you build should stay.

If you live by the Master's plan
That He laid out in His Holy Book for man,
The finished house will be strong,
And the time it will last, will be long.

A Father's Job

Father, when you look upon the world
What do you see?
Has Your creation progressed,
To where it ought to be?

Do you worry as all good fathers do,
About how Your children grow?
I believe as You watch us everyday,
There're some things You just know.

You know that most children
As they grow from day to day,
In trying to be different,
Try to do things their own way.

But fathers know when it's time
To change their child's direction,
Sometimes a gentle voice or a firm hand
Is needed for correction.

The world waits for You to come
To teach us how to live.
For You to know just what is needed
And You know just what to give.

Faithful Victory

God knew in His Being
That whatever He spoke,
Was definitely
Going to come true.
If you have that kind of faith
At work in your life,
You can have
That kind of victory too.

So ask of God
Who has all the power,
And to you
He will freely give.
Because He wants you
To be strong in faith,
And walk in His ways
And live.

Power Source

Faith is
The power source
To change your
Life for you.
Let it energize
Your mind
And your spirit
It will renew.

Raise me up

Why my Lord, can I not see,
What you have in store for me?
Help me Lord, to follow through
In whatever it is, you would have me do.
If I don't truly understand,
Please help me Lord to see Your plan.
And when my life starts to fade,
Help me not to be afraid.
Then when my time on earth is done
Raise me up, like You did Your Son.

The Moment

I'm at the end of me.
I can no longer carry
The burden of my life.
No one sees
The empty shell
Of my existence.
O God, forsake me not
In my hour of despair.
Let one glimmer of hope
Still reside deep down
Within my soul.
Give me a reason
To put one foot
In front of the other,
For my strength is gone.
I seek Your face.
To ask for Your Grace.
Have mercy on me.

If They Had Only Known

"Crucify Him, They Cried!"
O, but if they'd only known,
That He was the Savior sent from God,
But their hearts were as cold as stones.

The goodness in Him they could not see,
For they were truly blind.
They could see Him with their eyes,
But they were blinded in their minds.

I would hate to be one of that generation,
When they have to come before Him, on bended knee,
And they finally realize who it was,
That they crucified on that tree.

No Grudges

There's no way to undo
What's been done.
Yesterday's gone,
Never to return.
God will forgive you
If you do it His way,
Which is to forget about the past,
And start living today.

Always
(In Memory of Waymon)

There should always be
A glimmer of hope
In every situation.
As long as you
Know in your heart
That God is in control
Of His creation.

Breath of Life

The breath of life
Is a sacred thing.
It happens no where else
In the universe,
Except planet earth.
Yet, we take it for granted,
We do not give it
The reverence it deserves.
We waste this precious time
We are graced with,
Trying to fulfill
Some shallow selfish desire.
Seek God.

Compare

In six days
God made all
That there is.
And what,
You made
Five or six hundred dollars
This week?
Compare the two.
It ought to be enough
To make you meek.

Only Believe

The grave could not hold Him,
For he was the Father's Son.
He freely gave His life,
To undo what we had done.

Now the grave cannot hold us
Because He has already paid the price,
And as long as you believe He's Lord,
He will grant you eternal life.

Half Full

I feel like half a cup,
Half a glass,
Without you Lord
I'm fading fast.

How come that I
Could not see,
That without you Lord
Filled, I could not be.

You Too

God does what He pleases,
It must please Him that you are here.
Everything is done for His Glory,
His Word makes that very clear.

So what is it that you are here for,
Have you really given it much thought?
It must be very dear to Him
Because with His Son, your life was bought.

Ask God who gave you life,
What is His plan for you.
He will be sure to let you know
For Him, what it is you must do.

Whatever it is that He asks of you
He'll give you the strength to get if done.
He did it for the Lord Jesus,
And you're also considered His son.

Who Are We?

When you look into the mirror,
Who do you see?
Do you see someone that Christ died for,
As He hung upon that tree?

Have you ever considered,
Who you really are?
Do you know that you are a son of God,
Can your mind really reach that far?

God gave man control of
Everything that He made.
But when he sinned in the garden,
He gave that control away.

That is why He sent His Son
To die upon the cross,
For that was the only way,
To take back what was lost.

Why We're Here?

Father, You hover over Your creation
Like a new mother caring for her young.
With a tender heart to nurture,
A lion heart for protection,
A just heart for correction,
A broken heart of rejection.
Yet a heart so filled with love for us
That the whole universe
Cannot contain it.

Father, why can't man understand
His place in Your creation?
For he is Your ultimate handiwork,
Made in Your own image.
The only life You gave free will,
For whom You sacrificed Your Son
So we could be with You forever.
Yet most of us won't take the time
To find the purpose of our existence.

Father, please let man understand
You have a plan for every life You've created.
That we're not here for self indulgence,
But to do Your will upon the earth
Which is to show compassion to the poor,
To bring healing to the sick,
Redemption to the lost,
And that You gave us the ability to have the humility
To praise Your Holy Name.

My Prodigal Life

My life resembles that
Of the prodigal son,
From the ways of God
I've always run.

I wish I had known
That I couldn't leave,
For He had already planted
In me His seed.

As I grew older
I knew I'd been wrong,
So I raced to return
To the foot of His throne.

My joy overwhelmed me
As I understood,
That His love never left me,
For there's no way that it could.

Endure

To endure the struggle
Between good and evil
That plays out between
Your flesh and your soul,
You need to know Jesus,
Who'll give you the power
And the knowledge
To maintain some sort of control.

It won't always be easy,
Life never is,
But He will expect
The best you can do.
Sometimes you will win,
Sometimes you'll falls short,
But you can be certain
He will always be there for you.

My Life

To wish my life had been different
Is a waste of time.
My life is what it is,
But at least it's mine.

If I had done things different
I wouldn't be me.
I'm a product of my past,
For all to see.

God willing I can be different tomorrow,
If I don't like who I am today.
Bu turning over my life to Lord Jesus,
And getting on my knees to pray.

His Life He Gave

His life he gladly gave
For a world that was lost in sin.
It was in the Garden
That we gave up our Glory,
So we had to begin again.

He came down to live among us,
To show us how we should live.
We all need to follow His example.
It's not what you receive,
It's what you give.

So in all of life's situations,
Give some thought before you follow through.
It's not hard to be right
If you keep one thing in sight.
Just ask yourself, what would Jesus do.

These Chains

These chains can't hold us forever,
We must not lose our will to be free.
For it was just for that one single reason,
That our Lord gave His life on that tree.

Even though we may be locked up in a body,
We don't have to be locked up in our mind.
Just believe on our Savior, the Lord Jesus,
And in spirit, we can travel across time.

So in all things give God the Glory,
And it won't matter where we may be.
He'll move Heaven and Earth to come to our rescue.
For it is His will that we should be free.

Bended Knees

God got down on His knees
And put His hands into the clay.
He formed it into His own image
And created man that day.

I wonder what was on His mind
When He got ready to start,
Because I know He already knew,
That man would break His heart.

But He so loved us even then
That He went ahead with His plan.
For He knew that to save what He created,
He would send His Son down as a man.

The reason that we get on our knees
Before we seek His face,
Is to show Him that we understand
That we live only by His Grace.

In the Image of Me

People of the Earth
Listen to what I say.
I am the God of your fathers.
To know me you must pray.

Seek Me and I will come to you
To teach you what you must know.
I will give you wisdom and knowledge
To help you spiritually grow.

If you want to live forever
With Me out past the clouds,
You must surrender totally to Me,
And in your heart have no doubts.

Then I will be faithful to do what I say,
And in Me you can always believe.
Because when I created your very life,
I made you in the image of Me.

God Rules

There is no democracy in Heaven
The Lord God reigns supreme.
His every word is carried out to the letter
His Angels do not miss a thing.

There is no majority rule,
Nothing ever comes to a vote.
His every word is the law of Creation,
That's why His Book was wrote.

If you open it up and read within
You'll come to understand,
That God rules over His entire creation
Without any help from man.

Who Am I?

Who am I Lord?
Who am I?
What is my destiny?
Before the world
Was ever created,
You had a plan for me.

I need to know Lord,
I need to know,
What you would have me do.
Whatever it is,
I know I'll be blessed,
Because it comes from You.

Show Me How

Father, my heart's laid open
For You to see
How much I love You,
Come set me free.

For I long to live
A Holy life,
I've had too many tears,
I've paid too big a price.

Please help me Father
To understand,
How to live my life,
That You have planned.

Father, I promise You
That I'll not stray.
Please take my hand,
And show me the way.

His Will For Us

Try real hard to understand,
What God has really done for man.
Before God said, let there be.
There wasn't anything to see.

For everything was made for us,
And nothing came without His touch.
It was that way then, it's that way still,
Because everything that happens is by His will.

Man must one day come to know
That without Gods love, nothing will grow.
He just wants to help as any father would,
And He really loves us as only a father could.

The Father wants to be real clear,
That He will always be right here.
To do for you what He knows best,
Which is to help you enter His rest.

Don't Let Me

Father, be not
Far from me
In everything
I do.

Always open
My eyes to see,
That everything
Comes from You.

Do not let me
Stray too far,
From Thy
Loving ways.

Always bring me
Back to You,
Please don't let me
Fall from Grace.

Thy Will

Father, I want to do Thy will,
Please help me to understand.
It's my destiny You want me to fulfill,
Which is to be a righteous man.

I have to let You lead the way
In everything I do.
And in all thing never ceasing to pray
Which is how I stay in contact with You.

Great is Thy mercy towards me,
And Thy Grace I do not deserve.
That's why Thy will is my only plea,
And Thy will is to believe in Thy Word.

One Day

Who are we to question why
That some things happen that make us cry?
We cannot always understand
Why God lets these things happen to man.

We surely cannot always know
That some things happen to help us grow.
Mankind has got to one day see
That without God's love, we'll never be free.

I know that one day we'll climb above
The things that hinder us from His love.
And from that day forward, until the end of time,
God will not hesitate to say, these are Mine.

He Cares

Forever has no ending,
Neither does our Lord.
Not to do His Holy Will,
You cannot afford.

He only wants the best for you.
It is His only will.
He will bless you without measure,
If your heart you do not conceal.

Bring all things to Him in prayer,
It doesn't matter what you've done.
That is why He gave the world,
His only Son.

The Help We Need

Help me Father, to be strong,
For I don't want to do no wrong
It is my will to follow You,
Please show me what it is, that I must do.

When sometimes I fail to meet my goals,
I know my spirit You will console,
And by Thy Grace I'll be renewed,
And have the strength to follow through.

I wish all the world could see,
That to believe in You is all we need,
Because You would be faithful to send from above,
Blessings without measure, because of Your love.

When He Walked

If you want to live forever
You must understand,
That the Lord walked upon the earth
As a man.

He came to be an example
Of how we all should live.
It's not about how much you make,
It's about how much you give.

The Lord gave His very life,
And let them hang Him on a tree,
Because His blood was required,
To save both you and me.

So the next time you get a chance
To lend a helping hand,
Remember how much the Lord gave,
When He walked the earth as a man

With His Help

You will not live to see tomorrow,
If you don't make it through today.
So tune in with your spirit,
To what the Lord has to say.

He only wants the best for you,
It doesn't matter what you've done.
So open up you heart to Him,
And He will surely come.

He will give you wisdom and knowledge
To help you know what's right.
He will also give you His power,
For the evil one, you have to fight.

And in the end you will win,
If you follow His advice.
But get it right the first time.
Don't make Him tell you twice.

Totally Free

I can go the moon
Whenever I want to.
I can walk the rings of Saturn
Whenever I please.
I can go anywhere in creation
In an instant.
In my mind,
I'm totally free.

In the next life when I go
To live with Jesus
And I get the new body
He has for me.
I'll be able to do
All these things for real,
Because when I become a Spirit,
I'll be totally free.

Soldiers Of The King

Lift up your mighty voices
O ye soldiers of the King.
You will be victorious in battle,
So lift up your voices and sing.

Our Lord is mighty in battle
And worthy to be praised.
He will lead you on to victory
With your banners raised.

So fight the good fight and do His will
And the victory you will achieve,
Just do as all good soldiers do,
Which is in your King, believe.

His Friend

It's sad that mankind does not see
That his life was saved because of Calvary.
Man carries on from day to day,
Most don't even take the time to pray.

You should get to know Jesus Christ
Because it was for you, He paid the price.
He left His Glory with our Father above,
And came here to save you because of His love.

So get to know Him while you have the chance
For your life could be taken as quick as a glance.
Because you will answer for all of your sins,
It would be good to have Jesus consider you His friend.

The Love Of God

Man cannot grasp the love of God
Because it has no bounds,
It's so wide and long and tall and deep,
And everything it does surround.

We cannot run away from it
Even if we wanted to,
Because God will love us anyway,
It doesn't matter what we do.

Our Lord Jesus gave up His Glory
To come down and die for all men,
Because there is no greater love,
Than to give up your life for a friend.

So even though we don't understand
Why His love knows no beginning or end,
We know just as sure as night will become day,
That in His love, we can always depend.

Waiting On You

I sit and wait for the words to come
But yet my pen won't move.
I refuse to write just anything,
So Lord, I will wait on You.

If only I could be that way
In everything I do,
I wouldn't have need for anything
So Lord, I will wait on You.

My prayer is for the world to see
That they should do it too.
O how much better life would be,
If the world would wait on You.

His Blood

His blood dripped
From the cross
And fell upon the earth.
Since that was all
That was needed,
God took away the curse.

Because of that
Once again, His presence
We can enter in,
For just a few drops
Of His precious blood,
Has covered every sin.

The Prize

The Word will live
In the hearts of men,
If we open it up
And read within.

If you leave it lay
Upon a shelf,
You're hurting no one
But yourself.

Open it up
And be wise,
And set your sights
Upon the prize.

The prize we seek
Is Jesus Christ,
Who paid for your soul
With His very life.

Choices

There's a war going on inside you
Between the spirit and the flesh,
For control of your soul.
Who wins depends
On your use of the ultimate weapon
That God gave you.
That weapon is your free will
You get to decide the outcome,
Don't choose to lose.

The Thorn

The rose is so beautiful
And so pleasing to the eye.
The reason it grows upon the thorns
Is to buffer what could become pride.

Man is the ultimate creation
And the apple of God's own eye.
So sin came to be a thorn in his flesh,
To buffer what could become pride.

The Cross

Don't let the cross get lost
In the desires of your life.
For not to know its true meaning
Will not come without a price.

Help Me

Father, touch my heart and my mind,
Let me think Holy thoughts
Because sometimes this old world
Can get you down.
Please help me to understand
That You are always near,
And that with the life of Your Son
You bought my freedom
From the evil things of this world.
Now the only thing I have to fear,
Is missing out on the things
You have planned for me.
O Father, please help me to see.

While I'm Here

Father, send Your Spirit
To fill my mind.
Send Your love
To fill my heart.
Point me in the direction
Of paradise,
Give me the will
to start.

For it is only in You
That I will reach my goal,
Which you have always
Planned for me.
Which is to do Thy will
While I'm here on earth,
Then be with You
For eternity.

Our Conscience

We know when we do wrong
It's not like we do not know.
For God gave us a conscience
Where all we do doth flow.

It lets us know what's good or bad
Before we even act.
So we can't pretend we didn't know,
For we already had the facts

It's no coincidence how the mind of God
Has made everything work together.
I'm sure it's to keep us in line with His will,
So that our souls will live forever.

It Comes From Above

I'm just a pen
For my Father's words,
These are His thoughts
Not mine.
For all good things
Come from Heaven,
It's been that way
Since the beginning of time.

You think that Bell
Invented the telephone,
Or Edison invented the light?
I say the Father
Put these thoughts in their minds,
That it wasn't
Their insight.

When will man learn
That he has to have God,
Because all good things
Come from Him.
Creation is
A very structured place,
It was not built
Upon a whim.

A Single Tree

When God created everything,
It was as perfect as can be.
But shortly thereafter, everything changed
Because of a single tree.
But leave it to God
Who knows all that there is,
And all that will ever be.
Who put everything back
The way it was
Because of a single tree.

Rainbows

Rainbows only come after a storm
O they're such a beautiful sight.
But in order for you to see one,
There has to be a source of light.

Jesus is the light of this world.
In Him there is no night.
If you believe in Him with all your heart,
There will always be a rainbow surrounding your life.

Point Of Light

Lord, be a candle in the window for my soul.
Give me the right directions in which to go.
Let your light point the way,
From on my knees I pray.
For I know you will be there,
When I reach my goal.

His Love

Jesus will meet your every need
Just come to Him in prayer.
He stands before God and intercedes,
Hour after hour.

He will not be denied the goal,
Which the Father gave Him to do.
And that is the saving of all lost souls,
Which includes the likes of me and you.

So don't have too much pride to get on your knees
And thank your Father above
For having the wisdom to put Jesus in charge,
Because you cannot separate us from His love.

Jesus Is The Way

My Lord, My God,
Who created the stars.
Without You where would we be?
In the beginning
You gave us our lives,
And gave us our will to be.

Then in the garden
We gave up our Glory,
When we ate of the fruit of that tree.
Our spirits died that day
But You created a way
That again, our spirits could be free.

That way was Jesus
Who gave up His life,
In whom the Father was pleased.
He died on the cross,
So that none would be lost,
Which also includes you and me.

My Best Friend

Father, I trust in your judgment,
Let me walk in your will.
Give me of your spirit
Until I am filled.

Make straight my path before me.
Fill my heart with your love,
Pour out your blessings upon me,
From your window up above.

Let me know when I do wrong
Correct me with your hand.
For sometimes I will fall short
Because I'm just a man.

You made me in your image,
And you will love me until the end.
Not only are you my Father,
You're also my best friend.

The Center

The moon revolves around the earth,
The earth revolves around the sun.
If your life doesn't revolve around God,
You've lost even before you've begun.

God is the center of everything.
All things proceed from Him.
So if you don't make Him the center of your life,
Your future will be exceedingly dim.

So give God the chance to shine in your life
And you will never walk in darkness again.
Because He is the center of all creation,
And all things proceed from Him.

How Much You're Worth

Sun rays and moon beams,
Bring light to planet earth.
Jesus Christ brings light to your heart
To show how much you're worth.

Man is a special creation,
Unique in the whole universe.
We used to be covered in Glory
Before we fell under the curse.

But God in His wisdom created a way out,
In that we each must have a rebirth
So just let the Lord Jesus guide you through life,
And He'll show you how much you're worth.

Getting Through

God has done all He can
To make sure that you get through.
He sent down His Son to die,
The rest is up to you.

There comes a time in your life
To stand up for what you believe.
And if you don't, God will say
You have no part of "me".

But if you do, God will smile
On everything you do
And the Holy Spirit will make sure
That your soul will make it through.

Sinned and Saved

Father, you are
The Lord of all.
So why did we
Not heed Thy call?
Because we didn't
We had the fall.
That is why
We received the Law.

But that could only
Do so much,
And so we again
Fell out of touch.
Because in You
We didn't trust,
Again our lives
Became unjust.

Then You sent Jesus
Before our face,
And He gave His life
In our place.
Now of our sins
There is no trace,
Because the Lord has saved us
By His Grace.

The Mission

The light of Christ
Lights a world
Where darkness has prevailed.
He has not stopped shining
In the hearts of men
Ever since His hands were nailed.

His mission was
To come into the world,
So that through Him, none would be lost.
But for that to take place
And to bring in the era of grace,
He had to give His life upon the cross.

He gladly gave
His life for us.
It's what He's supposed to do.
And through that horrible death
He had on the cross,
His light came shining through.

Since That Day

God has not been hidden
Behind the veil,
Ever since the lord Jesus'
Hands were nailed.

He's been accessible
To you and me,
Ever since the Lord Jesus
Died upon that tree.

Now the Lord Jesus
Stands before the throne
And intercedes night and day,
For us alone.

From the sins we've committed
We are now freed
Because His precious blood
Is all God sees.

The Master Builder

Man needs to understand
That the foundation
For creation is love.
Everything that there is
Was built upon that,
Including the Heavens above.

God is the designer,
The Holy Spirit is the builder,
And Jesus is the perfect cornerstone.
For on Him our sins were laid,
And with His life He did pay,
So that we would have an eternal home.

Take Control

Father I'm through getting in your way.
I'm stepping aside to let You run my life.
Please don't ever take no for an answer from me.
I'm asking You, to make me do what's right.

You know what's best for me,
You can see things I don't.
I know you'll always do what's best for me,
You know if it's left up to me, I won't.

I give You full control to renew my mind,
So that I might fully understand
What Your purpose was in the beginning,
And what it was You expected of man.

So make me Father, do thy will.
I know it's not Your usual way.
My spirit is strong, but my flesh is weak,
Please take control of my life starting today.

The Garden

We can go back to the Garden
And worship like Adam and Eve.
That's why our Lord Jesus died,
To reverse Satan's lie,
That we were free to eat of that tree.

Again we can walk thru the Garden
With our Lord in the cool of the day.
And even though Satan tries,
We will never have to hide.
And of God, we'll never have to be afraid.

Minute by Minute

Every minute that you live
Could also be your last.
That is why it's so crazy,
To dwell upon the past.

Live right every minute,
Because you do not know,
When the God of all creation,
Will call for your own soul.

Then you will be judged for every minute
Of the life that you've been given.
That is why you should take this time,
To put your faith in the one who's risen

Second Chance

The rain fell and you could tell
That things would be different that day.
The sin of man had gotten out of hand,
And someone had to pay.

There is a price for everything,
Nothing in this life is free.
We are responsible for everything we do,
That's just the way it has to be.

But we are fortunate to serve a great God,
Who loves us more than we deserve.
He is always just, to leave us a way out,
If to Him only, we would have faith and serve.

So Noah got the call that day,
To save the Human Race.
It wasn't anything that he said or did,
It was just by the Father's Grace.

The future of man was saved that day,
Only by the Father's love.
Let's be thankful, it's still that way today,
That His love still comes down from above.

The Blood

The blood flowed from every wound
As He hung upon that tree.
It actually changed the course of life,
It was shed for you and me.

Now all throughout the course of time,
It covered every sin.
Because it's done its job so well,
God's presence we can enter in.

For God cannot see through the blood
That was shed for you and me,
Because it came, from His only Son,
As He hung upon that tree.

How Things Are

Have you heard an Angel sing?
Or listen to a butterfly
Flap its wings?
Have you ever felt
The earth move,
As it rides across the sky?
Have you ever seen the Lord,
Who's always standing by your side?

Just because things are not
Always as they seem,
Doesn't mean they can't be real,
We're not living in a dream.
The Lord is always there for you
Standing by your side.
To help you in your daily life,
If by His will you will abide.

The Church (1)

It's hard to write a poem about the church,
Because it's so difficult to make it rhyme.
Most people don't really understand
That the church is in your heart and mind.

Most people think it's that building down on the corner,
The one with the pretty glass and the high pointed steeple.
It comes from a lack of wisdom and knowledge
That the Body of Christ has always been the people.

Now even the people are divided into different groups,
You know, the Baptists, and Catholics and such,
And again the world does not understand
Because with the things of God, they're so far out of touch.

The reason there's so many variations
Is because we were created individually, and no one is the same,
Yet all together we are the bride of Jesus Christ
And we worship our Lords Holy Name.

You're God, I'm Not

Father, the difference
Between You and I,
Other than you're God
And I'm not,
Is that you love everyone
Regardless if they love You.
This I know is true,
Because You loved me
When I was so far away from You.
I could not see
The road I needed to go down,
To get back to You.
But, You turned night into day
And showed me the way,
Because You love me
More than I know.
You paid for my life.
Your Sons life was the price.
O Father, I'm so glad
You're God
And I'm not.

God Loves Us All

God is all around us.
He made everything we see,
He did not do it for Himself,
He did it for you and me.

God is still down here walking among us,
For His love for us has never changed.
It's His will that we get to know Him,
And when we need Him, call on His name.

He will be there to do what He should
To change our life and set our soul free.
Believe me when I tell you He wants to do this,
That's why He sent His Son to die on that tree.

Tell Me

My Father, My Lord
I know Your voice.
When You speak to me,
Please tell me the things
That I must do
To set my spirit free.

I will gladly do
The things I must,
To be with You one day.
Please help me Lord
To know what they are,
in Your name I pray.

They Know His Voice

The Good Shepherd waits
For His flock to come
So He can lead them home.
They gather around Him,
For they know His voice,
And they want no more to roam.

No Shadows

God has no shadow
For nothing around Him is dim.
Everything shines in His presence
Because all light proceeds from Him.

Around Him there is no darkness
For it cannot even get close,
Because He is the light of creation,
And the light of the Heavenly Host.

So if in your life you want no darkness
And would have it as bright as day,
Ask the light of creation to come into your heart,
By getting on your knees to pray.

Come Unto You

Jesus Christ came to die
For each and every sin.
And just so you could have eternal life,
He also rose again.

Now God the Father has given Him control,
Of all of life in the whole creation.
So if you want to meet Him face to face,
Your heart needs some preparation.

You need to study His Word and do what it says
And seek Him everyday.
But there is only one way to talk to Him,
You talk to Him when you pray.

So do all you can to understand
What it is He would have you do.
For if you be faithful in what you have learned,
The Lord will come unto you.

Walking With The Lord

My heart doth soar
To where the eagle flies.
When I understand
You'll never leave my side.

We'll walk this world
Through thick and thin,
Once I open my heart
And let You in.

I've set my mind
On things above,
I will not be separated
From Your love.

So please my Lord
Come unto me,
And by Your grace
Set my spirit free.

Wonder Why

Have you ever stopped to wonder why
The grass is green and not the sky?
Why the clouds are white, the ocean blue,
Have you wondered just who are you?

Have you ever really considered the reason
How everything has its place from season to season?
How a tree grows so tall from one little seed,
How the earth replenishes itself to fulfill all our needs?

Can you ever really understand
Why God does all these things for the one He called man?
If you think about it, it's not hard to fathom,
It's because we 're all descended down, from the one He called
Adam.

Adam's Heart

Have you ever wondered how Adam felt
When the weight of what he'd done
Had finally started sinking in,
When God put them on the run?

They had to leave God's paradise
And brave the wild beyond.
You know Adam's heart had to be breaking
Knowing he had given up his Holy bond.

He had to have known almost instantly
Being that his spirit was suffering in desperation,
From the knowledge of the fact that from the living God,
He would have to live his life in complete separation.

You know, I truly believe that Adam loved God
Until the day he died.
I also believe that from the day Adam sinned
God Almighty has cried.

Give God Control

God gave us a life
And He can take it away.
But you get to choose
How you will live until that day.

You don't know when it will be
That He will call for your own soul.
So be careful how you live your life
And who you give control.

You may think you're living a righteous life
But my friend don't be a fool.
For the evil one can be very deceiving,
He knows how to bend the rules.

So let God control every minute
Of the life He's given you.
And don't worry how things will turn out
He knows exactly what to do.

He Is Worthy

Worthy is the Lamb
To be praised.
Praise Him now
With you hands raised.
Worship Him in truth,
He gave His life for you.
Worthy is the Lamb
To be praised.

Blessed is His name
Upon the earth.
He came into this world
From virgin birth.
Follow Him and do no wrong,
His word will make you strong.
Blessed is His name
Upon the earth.

Glory, Glory
To His Holy Name.
He died for sins,
And not for fame,
He had to give His life for all,
Because of man's great fall.
Glory, Glory
To His Holy Name.

God's Gifts

God is all around you
If you take the time to look.
A lot of people think
He's only wrote about in a book.

They never take the time
To try to understand,
That God created everything
Just to be pleasing to man.

The flowers, the trees, the mountains, the seas,
Were all created for you.
God has made everything that there is
Just to give you something to do.

We must always remember to give thanks to God
For everything that he's done
For He loved us so very much
He even gave us His Son.

The Church (2)

The Church belongs
To Jesus the Christ.
He paid for it
With His very life.
It doesn't belong
To the Bishops, or the Pope,
Because in them
There is no hope.
If you want
Eternal life,
You have to kneel
Before Jesus the Christ.

The Little Things

To wake up with the ability
To enjoy a new day
That God has created
Is a gift, not a right.
You should be down on your knees
With your voice raised in praise,
To thank Him for His love
For without it, there would be no life.

His Love For Us

I thought that I had understood
God's love for us,
But there's no way I could.

For I cannot comprehend
That His love for us
Has no end.

There's just no words that can explain
How God's love for us
Has never waned.

God so loves us it's plain to see
That His only will
is to set us free.

To show that His love
We could always trust
God sent His Son to die for us.

His love for us you can never outrun,
Because we will always be covered
By the love of His Son.

The Price

God said
Let there be,
And it was,
Yet man can't see
That just because
Life was free,
There was a price,
Paid for you and me.

The greatest debt
That was ever due,
Was paid in full
For me and you,
The greatest price
It had to be,
was paid in full
On Calvary.

The Original Plan

When I look down on the earth I created,
Now that it's completely inhabited by man,
What I see is how far it has strayed from,
What it was I originally had planned.

I had created an actual paradise.
When I finished, I put man in.
Everything was absolutely perfect,
There was no death or sin.

Adam and I were having a great time.
Oh how I wish he had followed my instructions,
Which were to protect his family from the evil one.
But he didn't and it led to his destruction.

Ever since then, things have just gotten worse,
Which is why things are as bad as they are today.
That's why I'm getting ready to change it all back,
To what it was, that I originally had made.

The Holy War

There's a war in the heavens,
You must pick a side.
And by that choice
You will abide.

It's either right or it's wrong,
It's good or it's bad,
For there is no middle ground
to be had.

The choice is up to you
What will it be.
Will you stand with the Lord,
To set mankind free?

It will not be easy,
There will be loss of life.
Even on the Lord's side,
Yet we must fight the good fight.

Some will choose the losing side
Although it does not have to be.
For this war will be won
By the ones down on their knees.

Friends

Jesus walked across the sea
To get back to His friends.
He actually changed the law of nature,
To be with them again.

Think about what that means.
And if you get it right,
Jesus will travel all the way from Heaven
Just to be a part of your life.

He will change your entire being,
From the outside to deep within.
Because He came all the way from Heaven,
Just to be your friend.

Renewed

To watch the leaves
Fall from the trees,
Brings sadness to my soul.
I'm sure that's how the Lord feels,
When we drift from His protective fold.

In God's great plan
He made sure that man would forever be.
If you believe in His Son
You will rise from death,
As in springtime does the tree.

His Only Concern

Who are we to disbelieve
That God still saves today?
He always could be understood,
If you just had a little faith.

He will always do what He wants
It doesn't matter what we say.
We should understand why it is that man
Only lives because of His Grace.

For only then will we begin
To live the way we should.
He hopes that we will begin to see
That His only concern for us is good.

The Word

When they nailed Him to the cross
They did not understand
That the one they had just crucified
Was the Word in the shape of a man.

They couldn't have done things any different,
Because it was in God's great plan.
That in order to save what He had created,
He'd send the Word down to live among man.

While He was here, He daily walked the world,
Trying to make everyone understand,
That His life was the price of salvation,
And the reason eternal life was granted to man.

Now the Word is back up in Heaven,
And He's seated at the Father's right hand,
Where He never stops all night and day,
From interceding for every man.

Your Signature

Father, I'm sitting here
Watching the sun set,
And I'm in awe
Of the works of Your hands.
It doesn't matter
Which way I look,
Your signature,
is upon the land.

Even as I look inward
Into the feelings
Of my heart
and my mind.
Your signature
is there also,
As it's been
Since the beginning of time.

At My Cross

Jesus says, at My Cross you must decide
And by your choice you will abide.
You must stand up for what you believe,
For if you don't, you don't love me.

Some think my way of life is hard
But the enemy doesn't sleep so you have to stay on guard.
For he will surely steal your soul,
If you don't stay in contact with me and maintain control.

So just believe in me and you'll always win,
Because I've already died for all of your sins.
The choice is yours, what will you do?
Just ask of me, and I'll come to you.

God's Holy Word

God's Holy Word
Is all you need,
For power, strength, and faith.
It's been written down
Over the last four thousand years
And not one word has ever been erased.

No one can prove it wrong
And there's been
quite a few that's tried.
Because it was inspired by the Holy Spirit,
For whom it is impossible to lie.

So look in His Word
And learn all you can
About who the Father is.
And you will notice
From beginning to end
That the Father takes care of His.

The Illusion

Life without God
Has no substance.
It's not even real,
It's just an illusion
Of the evil one.
He would have you believe
That you are all you need
But please,
Come to your senses.
You know in your soul,
That control of your life
Must be turned over to God.

It's Never Changed

We should hide
Our face in shame,
The way we've treated
The one who's named
King of Kings, and Lord of Lords.
There's no way to save face,
It's only by His Grace
That His love for us has never changed.

So put away your foolish pride
Bow down and close your eyes,
And ask Him to change your heart and mind.
And if you are sincere,
And your heart and mind are clear,
Your life and His will forever be entwined.

Who We Are

God has made us who we are
Not who we want to be.
He also made the stars
And everything we see.

We must get to know ourselves
And why God puts us here.
He has a reason for everything,
Although to us it might not be clear.

That is why we have His Word
In which He wrote down His great plan.
But we have to open it up and read within
Before we can hope to understand.

Now if we're serious and open our hearts
And let His Spirit in,
Our minds will be totally changed,
And a new life we will begin.

Be Humble

"Humble thyself," it sounds so easy,
But in This World it's so hard to do.
The false pride of man gets in the way,
And clouds up our Heavenly view

Being humble is a big part of being Holy
It put you in the right state of mind.
The world says you must be exalted,
But god says, He will exalt you in time.

So humble yourself before the Lord
And in His Spirit do all that you can
To make this world a much better place.
For it is still the habitation of Man.

My Father' Son

The days of my life have drifted by
Like clouds up in the sky.
Some brought pain, some brought rain,
Which washed away my will to try.

But then I met Jesus who loved me for me.
It didn't matter what I had done
And now I know I will always be loved,
Because I'm also my Father's Son.

Source Of Secrets

The goodness of God has no measure
For no one can count that high.
All of creation was made just for us,
So we have no reason to cry.

All of life's secrets He put in His Word,
So that we would know how to live,
And the first thing to learn is that in order to receive,
We first must learn how to give.

Show Me What To Do

O Holy One of Heaven
Please listen to my plea.
I want to be with you forever
Please set my spirit free.

I will do all that it takes
To come and live with You.
I will surrender to You my life,
Just show me what to do.

It is Your Holy will
That all men should be free.
You put everything in Your Word
If we would just take the time to read.

And if we would, we would learn
Your love is always there
And that You will meet our every need
If we would just come to you in prayer.

Truly Believe

God says
If you let Me run your life
You'll never be the same.
I will teach you right from wrong
If you call on my Holy Name.
You will not have to do without
Because everything comes from Me.
Just believe in Me and have no doubt,
And I will truly set you free.

Don't Forget

Don't let the Cross
Get lost,
In the desires
Of your life.
For not to know
In your soul
It's true meaning
Will not come
Without a price.

A Certain Path

The earth follows a certain path,
On it's trip around the sun.
It will come back to where it started
When it's done.

Man may come from any direction,
On his trip to the Son.
But he will follow a certain path,
When it's done.

A Parent's Love

You know that special feeling you had
For your child when it was born.
When you held it close to your body,
To keep it safe and warm.

That's the feeling God's felt towards us
Ever since the beginning of time.
He has never hesitated to say,
These are mine.

But life goes on and all children grow,
And eventually want to leave home.
That's when you hope that all you have taught them
Will help them stand alone.

God thinks that way too, for He has guided our path,
Although we might not have known
And just as our parents, He will also be there,
In case you can't make it on your own.

Beginnings

"Listen, Listen,"
In the early morning dawn.
A new day is beginning,
The old one has gone.

Life is that way also
When you let God have control.
The old man dies away
And the new man takes a hold.

The Facts

My children, you walk around in darkness
In the middle of the day.
You choose not to listen
To what I have to say.

If you would take the time to know Me
You would understand the things I do,
Are only to ensure the quality of your life,
And to show My love for you.

I created you in the beginning
And I will judge you in the end,
If your spirit will live forever
On how you live your life, it does depend.

I Know

Father, the years
Come and go
But I know
You will be there.

The children we have conceived
Grow up and leave
But I know
You will be there.

I may lose my bet
On happiness,
But I know
You will be there.

I may fall
and lose it all,
But I know
You will be there.

And on my dying day
I'll still pray
Because I know
You will be there.

Stand In The Gap

Father, let revelation fall like rain
To water the mind of man
So that we may grow in the knowledge of You,
And in Holiness reclaim the land.

The prince of this world is trying to steal the harvest
That You have nurtured and raised,
But the Church of Your Son, Jesus the Christ
Will fight him face to face.

And in the end we will win
Because Your Word is true,
For You will give us the power, wisdom, and knowledge,
To accomplish what we must do.

The Vessel

Father, you are the potter
I am the clay.
Mold me Father
Unto thy way.

Make me a vessel
To do thy will,
Which is to hold living water,
Until I am filled.

Try me with fire
That I may come out strong.
Test me with temptation,
Help me to do no wrong.

And when at last You're finished,
Don't put me on a shelf
But let me fulfill my destiny
Which is the giving of myself.

Solid Rock

The rains will come
The winds will blow
To test the foundation you've laid
If you've built it
On the Lord Jesus,
Your foundation will surely stay.

Jesus is the solid rock
On which all buildings should begin.
Because if He's not
I can guarantee
Your life will come tumbling in.

He Thinks Of Us

My spirit sings unto the Lord
For what He's done for me.
That I may live He gave His Son
Upon the cross of Calvary.

His love for us has never waned
Throughout the course of time
The goal of saving all mankind
Is forever on His mind.

Only God knows what is to come
And what our lives will be.
We need to have faith in His love
And seek Him from our knees.

Skin And Bones

For forty seven years I've walked this earth alone
From day to day just skin and bones,
Because I have not let my Savior in
I've just been walking around, bones and skin.

But now I want to do what's right
Which is to let the Lord Jesus run my life
And if I follow His plan for Me
He's promised me a whole man I'll be.

Father And Son

Jesus stood at His Father's side
While He created all that there is
And although God said let's create man in Our image,
I'm sure the image was His.

I know the Father loved His Son that much,
For any father would.
And Jesus was His only Son
So He loved Him the way a father should.

Then the father asked Jesus to pay the price
That was due to save our souls.
Even though the price was His life, He never hesitated
Because pleasing His Father was His only goal.

That is why we get on our knees.
It's out of respect for what was done,
For the only reason we even have a life
Is because of our Father, and His Son.

Try Harder

What do you think God thinks
About how you live from day to day?
Do you think He's really happy,
About what you do and say?

The Word says that not a sparrow falls
In which He does not know
So how do you think He feels
When you refuse to spiritually grow?

He sent His Son to give His life
So you would not have to die.
And what do you do to repay that kindness?
You refuse to even try.

It's time to get on your knees and seek His face
And ask Him to direct your life.
Because if He was to come before you are ready,
You will have to pay the ultimate price.

The Promise

The world had been waiting
For four thousand years
For the one that had been promised to come.
Then one lonely night
Out with the animals
What had been promised was done.

God had sent His Son
Into this world
So that through Him we would not be lost.
His love for us must be more than we know
Do you really understand
The price that it cost?

Could you give up
The life of your son
For someone who doesn't even care?
That's what God did for us
So in Him put all your trust,
And take everything to Him in prayer.

The Father's Will

Fear not, say the Lord,
For it is Me,
For I have come
To set you free.
I gave my life
Upon that tree,
Now all you have to do is believe.

I came to do
The Father's will
And His Holy Word
Fulfill,
To let you know
He loves you still
And you sins
He has concealed.

Now all you have
To do is pray
And ask God to help you
Every day.
Be sure to hear
What He might say
And He will surely
Show you the way.

The Ultimate Expression

Singleness of soul
Was never meant to be.
It was not in
The great plan of creation.
Man was designed for companionship,
Both spiritual and physical.
To be whole, we must have a relationship,
With both the Creator,
And the opposite gender.
Anything less causes loneliness,
And loneliness only leads to despair.
We can avoid that vortex
With the use of
What holds Creation together
Which is our ability
To give and receive
The ultimate expression
That being Love.

A Father's Love

As I look up into the midnight sky
I cannot help but wonder why
Of all the worlds that I can see
You chose the earth to let man be.

Now we've been here six thousand years
We live our lives, we have our fears.
And You supply our every need
which even includes the air we breath.

Why is man so dear to You,
That You do all that You do?
You did not even withhold your Son,
It was because of us that it was done.

Help me Father to understand
Why so great a love is shown to man.
Can it be the same above,
As it is on earth, just a Father's love?

His Holy Name

"Jesus", it's just a name
But oh what a name it is,
There is so much awesome power in it,
Because the name was His.

For four thousand years it had been promised
That the Anointed One would come,
And when He came they named him Jesus
Because He was His Father's Son.

After He died, He went back to the father,
And things have never been the same
Because before He left, He gave us the authority
To use His Holy Name.

The Era Of Grace

A new day dawned
In the heart of man,
When Jesus came to earth,
The Father had sent
His only Son
To show us how much we're worth.

The era of Grace
Had come upon the world
Although we did not deserve,
But His mercy towards us
Endures forever,
As it plainly states in His Word.

God's love towards us
Has no end
Why is it man can't see,
That we were created
To be one with Him
It's what our spirit needs.

So give your life unto the Lord,
No matter what the cost
For if you don't
Your eternal spirit
Will forever and ever be lost.

Salvation Plan

Father, your ways are perfect
My ways are not.
With the life of Your Son
My soul has been bought.

His will was your will
Our salvation was your plan.
Jesus freely gave His life
For the salvation of man.

So to show some respect
We bow down on our knees
And give thanks to you,
Who answers our pleas.

The Way I Must Go

Father, make straight the path I follow through life,
That I may never have to look around a curve.
Help me to follow the directions
That You laid out for me in Your Word.

I'm trusting you to guide me through safely
When I come upon some of life's rocky roads,
Because sometimes the only way to get through,
Is to have someone help carry the load.

Father, when I reach my final destination
And look back on the way I came,
Help me to understand that I made it,
Only because I believed in Your Name.

The Victory

Arise O Lord
And deliver me
From the hands
Of the enemy.

He tried to steal
My very soul
But You came to me
And made him go.

Help me Father
To stand the test,
For the evil one
Will never rest.

If I keep
My mind on You,
He won't be able
To break through.

For the evil one
Cannot stand
Against my God
Or against Your man.

And through it all
I will win
Because in You
There is no sin.

False And True

Some people think
You get one shot at life,
But that's not right
I say
You get a new chance, everyday.

Some people think
That life's not fair,
That no one cares.
It's not true,
God loves you.

Holy Spirit

The Spirit moves
Upon the hearts of men
To check and see
What is within.

If He finds
A Godly seed
He will nourish it
With whatever it needs.

He will not be
Denied His goal,
To free us all
And save our souls.

So when you pray
Get on your knees
And let the Spirit
Do what He pleases.

Before

The world was
A different place
Before Adam
Fell from Grace.

There was no death
There was no sin
Before he fell
And let it in.

There was only life
And happiness,
Because the world
Was truly blessed.

Before man
Received the curse,
Our God walked
Upon the earth.

The Son

The Son
Wants to shine
In every life
Where darkness
Has a hold,
Because once you
Let the Son in,
The darkness
Has to go.

Forgive Me Lord

Forgive me Lord
For I have sinned.
Please help start
My heart to mend.

Because of Thy Grace
All I have to do
Is say, forgive me Lord,
And in my heart be true.

I know You will be faithful
To come unto me
To do what Your Word says,
And set me free.

We're Still The Same

Man has been around
For six thousand years,
And yet we haven't changed.
We might be a little
More comfortable,
But yet we're still the same.

When will man learn
That he has to have God
In order to be truly whole?
We must continue to pray,
All night and day
And make loving God our only goal.

That's Why

God created
Heaven and earth.
He was also in charge
Of the Virgin birth.
The first was done
So man could be,
The second was done
To set man free.

O Lord

Come into my life O Lord
And truly set me free.
For without You in my life O Lord,
I have no will to be.

Only in You is there life O Lord
For there is no other one.
Because all life comes from the Father,
And was given to the Son.

The Things I Do

O Lord God
Why art thou
Concerned with me
And the things I do?
For I have always
Come up short
In trying to serve You.
You have never left me
Nor forsaken me,
Because Your Word is true.
That is why,
I will always try to do what
You would have me do.

The Mind

Your mind
Is an expanse
Of space
That should only
Be filled
By God,
Because
No one else
Knows what
It's capable of.

The Truth

Jesus came to teach and save
And to do the Father's Will.
All the words of the Prophets of old
He also came to fulfill.

No one understood who He was
Or what He had come to do.
Because of the evil in them, they could see,
That He was God's Word of Truth.

The reason they had to kill Him,
Was the truth they could not bare
For they had broken their covenant with God,
And their spirits were in despair.

Man cannot change the plan of God,
So the Truth was brought back to life.
In His blood a new covenant was made,
Because he had paid the ultimate price.

Now if you today want to understand the Truth,
Open God's Word and read within.
For He will give you the wisdom and knowledge of Creation,
If you will confess to Him all of your sins.

The Spirit's Work

O precious Holy Spirit
You bring knowledge to my mind,
Which I turn into wisdom,
Which helps to keep me in line.

You were sent to change the world
By changing the hearts of men.
You don't do it from the outside,
You do it from within.

You've carried on the Father's work
For the past two thousand years,
By changing our hearts, by renewing our minds
And comforting all our fears.

You will not be denied your goal
To bring Christ to planet earth.
You'll do that one soul at a time
By showing us how much we're worth.

Follow That Cloud

Father, send your fiery cloud before me
To show me which way to go.
You know I'll gladly follow,
Even to places I do not know.

And when it stops you know that I'll
Stand firm right where I am.
Then when it starts, you know that I
Will follow it once again.

Father, I know in my heart it's you in that cloud
And you will not lead me to do no wrong.
And if I follow it daily, never leaving its path,
It will lead me to the foot of your throne.

Jesus Cried

The Word says Jesus cried.
Have you ever wondered why?
I don't think it was for Lazarus
Because He was going to bring him back to life.

I think it was because the plan for man
Had gotten so far out of hand.
He had helped to create us in the beginning,
So He knew our potential
And how far we had fallen.

So be glad He came.
Praise His Holy name.
Thank Him for His tears.

Partners

Walk with me Lord
Down life's lonely road.
Go with me Lord,
And help carry the load.

Stand with me Lord
When troubles come.
Let's stand back to back,
And fight the evil one.

The Lord does not promise
An easy free ride.
But the Lord does promise,
He'll always be by your side.

Paradise Again

I sit and watch the world
Hoping to one day see,
It turn from its evil ways
And return to Me.

When it does, I will be faithful
To make it Heaven on High.
I'll remove the curse I put on it,
And return it again to Paradise.

Colors

God made everything in color,
From the flowers to the trees.
And just so things wouldn't be boring,
He also included you and me.
Now he did not forget the animals,
For they are colorful too.
Color doesn't bother them,
Why should it bother you?

Changed

They followed Him up the mountain,
Not knowing what they'd see.
Then within the blink of an eye,
He was changed into the light of eternity.

You never know when you follow the Lord,
What He'll let you see.
But you can be sure whatever it is,
It will help set your spirit free.

Then in the end when our life is over,
And He calls us by our name,
If we have followed Him faithfully
In the blink of an eye, we will also be changed.

Be Holy

As water falls upon the earth
And brings life to everything,
Let your words fall upon my mind,
And bring forth the Holy things.

Father, I don't want to do no more wrong
Please help me carry this through.
I know I can't do this on my own,
Because my strength comes only from you.

I surrender to you my very life
To mold and shape for me.
And if I keep focused only on you,
I'll be as Holy as can be.

The Light Of Christ

God lit a spark in our darkened hearts
That still shines bright today.
It travels from generation to generation
For it will never fade away.

The source of that light is Jesus Christ
Who turns darkness into day.
He will light up the path you must travel
So that you will never have to be afraid.

His Ways

Fear the Lord and live.
Walk in His ways,
Learn to freely give.
From His ways do not stray.

These are the secrets to life.
Do them and live long.
For you will endure no strife
And you will not want to do no wrong.

The Source Of Life

Father, you reached down and touched my heart,
Now I will never be the same.
You became so real to my mind,
That I know it was from you it came.

You opened up my eyes
To let me see that from above,
Comes the source of all life.
And that source is your love.

How Far

How far away is Heaven
Someone asked me today.
I told them it's only the distance
Between your heart and your mind,
When you get on your knees to pray.

The Great Lie

I don't believe in Mother Nature,
I believe in Father God.
Satan wants you to believe
That everything just evolved.

Evolution is the biggest hoax
That's ever been put over on man,
Since Satan talked Eve into eating of that tree,
By telling her it would help her to understand.

As it was way back then, it's still that way today.
To deceive man, Satan will always try.
It's just who he is, he knows nothing else,
For he is the father of and is the greatest lie.

Words

Forever is a word,
Used to describe
The length of time
That you will be with
Or without God,
Depending on what
You believe in your mind.

Never is another word,
Used to describe
How long it will be
That you will have to
Live without God,
If you believe His Son
Gave His life on that tree.

Understand

Understand that God
Works through man.
You don't always
Get divine revelation,
It might be a stranger
That keeps you from danger,
but Gods word
Will reach its destination.

It's All I Know

Mere words cannot explain
The love God has for man.
There's nothing in our vocabulary
That could make us understand.

His love for us knows no limits
No one knows why that is.
There's no way that we deserve it,
But yet He freely gives.

He sent His Son to planet earth
To cover all our sins.
It was the way to ensure
That Heaven we could enter in.

When I get there, I'm going to ask Him
Why He loves us so.
And I fully expect Him to answer,
"It's the only thing I know."

Which Road

The road to Heaven is like an old country road,
Filled with ruts, bumps, and curves.
The only way to follow it safely
is by staying in God's Holy Word.

The road to Hell is like a new super highway,
Perfectly straight and smooth as glass.
If you follow its signs which are the wisdoms of this world,
Your trip will be exceedingly fast.

Surrender Me

Father, look into my heart
And know my heart is true.
It's you I want to serve,
Please show me what to do.

I'm here to do thy will
Please help me to see,
That in order to serve you,
I must surrender me.

Me Too

To know that I will one day see
Me Father face to face.
And not from anything that I've done,
It is only by His grace.

My Father cares so very much
About the life I live.
I don't have to ask for anything,
Because He freely gives.

He truly loves me so very much
It doesn't matter what I've done
Because of my Savior, the Lord Jesus Christ,
I'm also considered His son.

You Can't Hide

For three days was Jonah
In the belly of the whale.
Even though a lot of people
Think it's just a fairytale.

But it's true it doesn't matter
What it is that you heard.
For it wasn't, it wouldn't be
In God's Holy Word.

Now the whale brought Jonah,
And put him on the land,
Where he still had to do
What it was God had planned.

So just remember if there's something
That God wants you to do,
Just do it, don't make Him
Come looking for you.

The One I Serve

Father, you bless me every day
Even though I do not deserve.
That's why you are my God,
And the only one I serve.

I will not forget your grace
When I get on my knees.
I will praise your Holy name
For it's you I want to please.

Oh please help me to see
That you are the only way.
Oh help me Father to do thy will,
In your Holy name I pray.

Inner Peace

Before you lift your hands to Heaven,
Look inward to your heart.
If you have not made your peace in there,
Then that's the place to start.

When you have done all that you can
To make your peace within,
Then lift your hands to Heaven,
So your healing can begin.

The Power Source

Dear God, help me in this hour
To do Thy Holy will.
From you comes all my power,
In you I am fulfilled.

God, I know it's you I need
To live from day to day.
In you my soul is freed,
I will never be afraid.

The Goodness Of God

He lifted me up into His presence
From where I had bowed down on my knees.
And the first thing to catch my attention was
That goodness was visible, as far as you can see.

No one had to do without it,
For it was so easily found.
Because there was so much of it,
The whole creation it did surround.

So don't be afraid to ask for some,
For you shall freely receive.
And the best time to ask God for some,
Is when you are down upon your knees.

These Times

Father, are my prayers
Getting through to you?
I try to be as good
As I should, most of the time.
It's hard to see
Your will for me,
When I try myself
Without your help,
Which I do sometimes.
Father, please help me
To see the need, to do what's right
And put you first
In my life all the time.
May I always know
In my heart and soul,
That the Lord of my life
Is your Son Jesus Christ,
For the rest of the time.

Do Not Tarry

Lord, do not tarry long
Before you come to take us home.
For we watch, and wait, and hope to see,
The days our souls will be set free.

O how we wait for that day to come
Knowing thy will must be done.
The whole world shall wake by a shout so loud,
As you descend in all Glory from the clouds.

Yours you will take home with you that day,
So be ready, always, watching and always pray.
For no one knows when that day will be,
O come Lord, we're waiting, upon our knees.

He Cannot Be Defined

God is only limited
In the scope of your mind.
In the realm of creation
He cannot be defined.

Man thinks he is so intelligent
But it's just a prideful lust.
How easy it is for us to forget
That God made us out of dust.

Even in our vast imagination
We cannot even begin to conceive,
The ultimate power and wonder of God,
And the reason He caused us to be.

So don't try to put God in some little box
That you've created in your mind,
Because He is the Almighty, who created everything,
And He cannot be defined.

Last Chance

A new day dawns
In the life of men
We get a chance
To begin again.

Yesterday is gone
Never to return.
Today you get
A new chance to learn.

What will you do
With this precious time,
Will you use it
To expand your mind?

Or will you let it
Just fade away,
Hoping that you
Will see another day?

Don't bet your soul
That tomorrow will come,
If God calls for your life
His will shall be done.

And you will have lost
The last chance you get,
To know of His love,
And to enter His rest.

Flowers Don't Lie

Trees don't bribe,
Flowers don't lie,
Animals don't sin, only men.
The reason God
Put man in charge
Is his brain is large.
That's why we're
Supposed to do
What He told us to,
But we didn't.
So sin began
To destroy man,
And his soul
Lost all control.
Something had to be done,
So He sent His Son,
To die for us
And break the curse.
Now man has the chance
Where he can dance
In Heaven above
Because of God's love.
But we have to do
What He wants us to
And that's to give our life
To Jesus Christ.

Freedom

Freedom is
The God given
Right to decide,
That God gave
You the right
To decide.
So why not
Decide to be
Free from sin,
And begin again?

Lucky Me

Father, I thank you
That by your infinite wisdom
I have been born into this age,
Because I don't think
I would have made it long
If I'd been born
Before the era of Grace.

I'm sure my flesh would have been
As weak back then
As it is today,
But back then
I would not have had the luxury
To say, forgive me Father,
In Jesus name I pray.

The Reason (1)

Six thousand years ago
God created all that there is.
He gave it to man
And said it was his.

All that there is
He gave it for free,
Saying you can do what you want,
Just don't eat of that tree.

He said, I'm giving you fair warning
And you know I can't lie.
If you eat of this tree
You will surely die.

Now the devil comes along
Disguised as a snake,
He tricked the innocent woman
And from the tree she did eat.

She gave it to Adam
And he ate of it too.
That's why Christ had to die,
To save me and you.

The Reason (2)

I know you hold my hand Lord
As my mother used to do,
To keep me from all danger,
And to show You love me too.

We never grow too old
As not to need that kind of love.
If we can't get it here on earth,
We can always get it from above.

You said, I will never leave you, nor forsake you
And that I know is true.
For with Your life, You paid the price
Because blood was what was due.

So now we're free to live our lives
Without fear from what's to come.
And that's because You loved us so
And did what had to be done.

My Prayer

My God, My God,
Where art thou
In my hour of despair.
My soul longs for
The gentleness of Thy touch.
My heart is heavy,
I cannot carry
This load alone.
Father, reach down
From thy Heavenly
Abode,
And fill my spirit
With Your very nature.
May we intertwine
Like vine and arbor,
I shall praise
Thy name forever.
AMEN

Purpose

The years come and go
It's our responsibility to grow.
Not just to live up to
Others expectations.

There is purpose in being
Not just in seeing,
What you can accumulate
In this life.

For you are your Father's Son,
The One and only One.
So act like an heir
Of the One who created all that there is.

He Will Be There

Loneliness is a soulful thing,
for there is no one in which to share.
So all your thoughts stay deep inside
Which leads your heart and mind to despair.

But the Lord said you don't have to be lonely,
You don't even have to have a care.
For I will never leave you, nor forsake you.
My love will always be there.

So give your mind and heart to Him
And with you He'll always be fair.
But remember the Lord is a jealous God,
And your love, He does not want to share.

My Father's Knee

I wonder what it will be like
To set upon His knee,
And ask Him all those questions,
And have Him answer me.

He will look with love into my eyes,
As I look upon His face.
And with only the love a father has,
All my fears He will erase.

O how I long for that day to come,
when I can lay my head upon His chest.
And tell Him, I love you, and thank you Father,
For allowing me to enter into Thy rest.

In Memory Of Opal

My mother taught me all I know
About the Christian way.
It wasn't anything that she said,
She just lived it everyday.

She never preached to anyone,
About their sinful ways.
She always led by example,
And always had time to pray.

But now that she's gone, I miss her so much,
That I've often gone astray.
Then I look back on her life, and it helps me to do right,
Because she taught me to do it God's way.

Your Desire

Father, some live and die
And never know your love,
For lack of wanting correction
From above.
But I know it's your desire
To make us all an heir,
If only we would live
In Your love.

Repent

O nations of the earth
Listen to what I say.
It's time to return to God
For you might not get another day.

The earth trembles in agony,
Because your sins are too great to bear.
The ground is covered in so much blood
That even God refuses to care.

You do not even care for one another,
So why should God care for you?
Even though He is patient and merciful,
His justice and judgments are true.

So nations, bow down before God's throne
And pray it's not too late.
And if you sincerely change your hearts and minds
You could also change your fate.

Our Glory

Father, the Word says You created us in Your image.
To me that means we were created to be just like You.
Father, if we were created to be God-like creatures,
Then why did we give up our Glory and not remain true?

Most people just don't understand
That in the garden, it was our Glory we lost.
For that was the element that made us just like You,
yet man still doesn't understand what it cost.

We were covered in Glory just like You,
And in that way we were the same.
Then for some reason, Adam chose to go a different route
And we lost the right to be called by your name.

Now we have to die to get back our Glory,
But only if we live the right way.
And if we do, You have faithfully promised
That it will again, be like it was that very first day.

My Plan

I cannot be denied My goal
There's no reason to even try.
My plan for man will succeed
So there's no reason for you to cry.

I let Satan have this moment
Just to prove that he was wrong.
The lesson being that the sin in your heart,
Will keep you away from My Throne.

I will cleanse Creation from his evil ways,
And all who have followed him.
In order to survive, you must keep your eyes on Me,
And a new way of life, we will begin.

The Trinity

When you pray unto the Father
He refers it to His Son
Who relays it to the Spirit,
Who makes sure that it gets done.

Then sometimes it works in reverse
But it makes no difference you see
For either one of them is God.
They are the Trinity.

His Hallowed Ground

You walk on Hallowed Ground
Although you may not know,
For God created all the earth
And made it grow.

He walked daily through the garden,
Between the flowers and the trees.
He loved the cool of the day so much
I'm sure that's why, He created the breeze.

Everything still belongs to Him
Although He lets us use it
We should watch how we use the earth,
And be careful not to abuse it.

God still walks around today,
To see what's still around
And to check and see how we're treating
His Hallowed Ground.

Study My Word

My son, read my Holy Word
Seek out the truth within,
If you will store it in your heart
A new life you can begin.

You have to really want it badly
I will not force it upon you,
If you can understand who I am,
You will know my word is true.

You might understand it instantly
Or it could take all your life.
It doesn't matter to me which one it is
As long as you get it right.

And if you seek it diligently
With a heart that's pure,
I'll promise you because I am God,
That your eternal life will be secure.

Our God

God has always been
And God will always be.
My mind has no concept of that,
It's just too high for me.

We need to keep God in perspective
Because we don't really understand
That He actually created the Heaven and Earth,
And it was out of the dust that He made man.

God is our Heavenly Father,
And for us He has a great love.
Everything that we have and everything that we need
Is sent down from our Father above.

So praise God and give Him the Glory
For everything you have received,
And know in your heart He will always be there
To fulfill your every need.

My Friend Jesus

When you think your road
Has come to an end,
That's the time to ask Jesus
To become your best friend.

You will find you never new
What life is about,
And your mind will be filled
With nothing but doubt.

But Jesus will be there
To fulfill all your need,
Never again in silence
Will you have to plead.

He's always as close
As a thought in your mind,
Because with the Lord Jesus
There is no meaning to time.

His Breath

The invisible force of life
That flows through us all
Is the same,
It never changes.
So why are we so different?
If we could only
Let it transform us
Into what we should be,
We might understand
The true meaning
Of our existence.

Invest In Jesus

Life will past you by
If you don't enjoy the ride,
And I have found there is no pleasure,
Without the Lord.

On earth nothing will last,
And you can't dwell on the past,
So you better invest in something
You can afford.

So invest in Jesus Christ
Who for you gave up His life,
It wasn't for anything,
That you had done.

He did it because the Father asked,
It was done to erase your past.
That's why life without Him,
Would be no fun.

One Step at a Time

Father help me follow in Your footsteps
Even though, them, I cannot see,
For if I'm truly following You,
I know they're right there in front of me.

Help me to take one step at a time
Because that is what You do,
For if I get into a big hurry,
I'll run right over You.

Then I'll be out front all by myself,
With no one to guide my way.
That is when I'll be at my weakest point,
And for anyone I'll be easy pray.

So Father please stay always one step ahead,
For I know Your path is true.
Please help me to take just one step at a time,
Always staying in You Shadow behind You.

The Cost

We chose to live
With every breath we breathe.
Jesus chose to die,
And let them hang Him on a tree.

They thought that they took His life,
But if they only knew
That He freely laid it down,
To save both me and you.

So give some thought to who you are
And who you ought to be,
Because there was a price paid for you,
And every breath you breathe.

His Precious Love

Fear not my children
And follow me.
For have I come
to set you free.

It's not as hard
As people say.
All you do is
Believe and pray.

If you keep your mind
On the things above.
You cannot help
But feel My love.

You know My love
Is all you need.
To shape your mind
And set you free.

In Awe

Father I stand in awe
Of everything that you've done,
From the creation of all life
To the giving of You Son.

You've held nothing back,
Although I do not deserve.
That is why You'll always be,
The only God I serve.

Listen

If you listen real close
With your heart
You may hear the calling
Of the Lord.
If you're listening with your ears
You will miss it
And that you cannot afford.

For He's calling you
To repentance
Which you need
To save your soul.
And if you
Do not hear Him,
To Heaven you will not go.

Father, Please

Father, I cannot contain
My desire to feel
That you have taken control
Of my life.
From my knees I cry out
For Your tender mercy.
The Word says:
"Seek and you shall find."
I've sought but still I feel
An emptiness of Your presence.
Could it be a lack of faith
On my part?
I think not because I truly believe.
O Father, please help me to see
How much You love me.

Have No Fear

If you believe in God
Never be afraid.
Fear is of the devil
It has never been God's way.

Nothing can make Him tremble
Because all there is He made.
It's the ones that are not in His Will,
And the devil who should be afraid.

Mom

My mother died and went to Heaven
When I was just a young man.
At that time
I didn't understand.

I asked the Lord why,
Why it had to be.
But because of the way I acted,
He never answered me.

Now that I'm older and wiser
I'm finally beginning to see.
That the reason He took her to Heaven early
Was so she could intercede for me, personally.

God Says

I'm near even before you think of Me
Although you cannot see.
If I were to really open your eyes
What you would see you could not believe.

The natural and the spirit world,
Are forever entwined.
The natural you see with your eyes,
The Spirit you see with your mind.

In order to look into the Spirit world
You have to stay focused on Me.
And if I see that your heart is right,
I'll let you peek in and see.

But I cannot let you look that long,
No matter what it's worth.
Because then you would never be happy again,
Having to live upon the earth.

Instead Of Me

When I look upon the cross
You know what I see?
I see the place my Savior died,
Instead of me.

When I pray unto the Father
I get down on bended knee.
I do this because my Savior died,
Instead of me.

When I sing unto the Father,
I do it all with glee.
I do this because my Savior died,
Instead of me.

Now I'm going to live forever
Because my soul is free.
This I know because my Savior died,
Instead of me.

Printed in the United States
79160LV00003B/115-234